# POWER EDITING FOR FICTION WRITERS

## Carolyn V. Hamilton

*Power Editing For Fiction Writers*
ISBN 978-0-9909664-3-2

www.carolynvhamilton.com

Swift House Press
7380 S. Eastern Avenue, Suite 124-216
Las Vegas, Nevada

# INTRODUCTION

Congratulations!

You've completed the first draft of your novel!

You think *that* was work? Get ready for EDITING! This is where your major work begins.

POWER EDITING is not just about making sure the words are spelled correctly and the grammar is correct.

POWER EDITING is looking at every aspect of your writing—from your initial story idea, through the telling of your story, to how you craft your sentences.

Well, yes, and spelling and punctuation, too.

**This book is for fiction writers who plan to indie publish (we used to call it "self-publishing," but now we're "*indie*-publishers.")**

I've had writers in my classes say, "Oh, I'll just hire an editor to edit my book."

Really?

And what is your budget for that?

Professional editing is not cheap. Not only that but, to cover all the bases, you will likely need to hire *two* people, a Developmental or Content Editor and a Copy or Line Editor. Later on in this book I'm going to explain to you the difference.

If you want to hire an editor—and when you feel you are *completely finished* with your manuscript you should pay a qualified person to look at the work—you will need to budget anywhere from $3/page to $40/hour. And that's the *low* end.

You only have to google "average editing costs" to verify what I'm talking about.

But YOU can control the expense. By editing as well as possible yourself, you can drastically reduce professional editing costs.

It just makes sense—to me, at least—that the less work your editor has to do, the less expensive it will be.

In this book, *Power Editing For Fiction Writers,* I want to make the editing process easy for you. I want to help you craft your novel to the highest possible level. I want you to feel confident in your writing, and to impress your reader with your storytelling *and* the professional presentation of the words on each page.

I've kept this book as simple and concise as possible, with practical information you can APPLY RIGHT NOW to your manuscript. That's why this is *not* a 75,000-word, 300-page reference book.

*Power Editing For Fiction Writers* is arranged in two sections:

**Part One** addresses the elements of your story, and how you have used them. **Part Two** addresses your writing, the grammar and word use part.

I'm going to show you how to critique your manuscript based on your story's concept and characters, action and plot points.

I'm going to share with you a fantastically easy editing system, how to use powerful word arrangements called "rhetorical devices", and of course, the **NUMBER ONE SECRET** I promised you to POWER UP your writing today!

I'm going to challenge you to tear your manuscript open to ruthlessly critique every single part, and I'm going to show you how to do that in an easy-to-learn, non-scary way.

So, grab a fresh cup of coffee and let's jump in and get going!

# TABLE OF CONTENTS

## PART ONE: YOUR STORY

## PART TWO: YOUR WRITING

# PART ONE: YOUR STORY

### CHAPTER 1 – The "High Concept"

Is your story "High Concept"? What does that mean? And how can you tell?

Hollywood screenwriting expert Hal Croasman is a master at explaining High Concept.

So what is High Concept?

Hal says this is the "big idea of your story." It's what will—you hope—set your book apart in the ever-increasingly competitive literary marketplace.

HIGH CONCEPT has also been described as a type of artistic work that can be easily pitched with a simply-stated premise. No one is clear on who coined the term "high concept" but it's been around in the film industry for several years.

And HIGH CONCEPT applies to books as well.

A clear example of high concept is the movie *Snakes on a Plane*. I don't have to tell you any more about what the story line is. You can easily envision a plane full of snakes. *Eeeeeuh!*

In his novel *The DaVinci Code*, author Dan Brown explored the premise that in an alternative religious history kings of France were descended from the secret marriage of Jesus Christ to Mary Magdalene. The result was a blockbuster.

J.K. Rowling hit it big with her high concept of "gifted" British schoolboys like *Harry Potter* attending a private school for magic.

Author Charlain Harris went HIGH CONCEPT with her Sukie Stackhouse vampire series. Vampires out of the closet? Out in the open? In Louisiana? Where they can buy a six-pack of blood at Seven Eleven? *True Blood* is definitely high concept.

With her blockbuster book, *Fifty Shades of Gray*, E.L. James took the concept of the modern erotic romance novel to another level by adding a major plot element that many might consider pornographic: dominance, bondage and submission. *Fifty Shades of Gray*, by the way, was originally indie-published by James as an e-book.

With a dynamic HIGH CONCEPT you increase the chances that your readers will be ecstatically entertained, and that maybe—just maybe—Hollywood will want to make your book into a movie or TV series.

Hal Croasman tells us, "A novice writer with a high concept stands a better chance of selling his/her book than a mid-list author without a high concept."

That's good news, right?

To tell if you have a high concept story, ask yourself the following questions:

Is my story different from everything else in my genre? How?

Is there a universal theme readers can identify with? Love? Hate? Jealousy? Desperation? Revenge?

Does my story have instant emotional appeal?

Can I tell my story in one sentence in a way that my reader can instantly visualize it? Remember *Snakes on a Plane*.

Here is a one-line example explaining the high concept of my murder mystery, *Magicide*:

*When a famous Las Vegas magician is murdered, all the suspects are magicians.*

Now, I don't want you to get hung up thinking these are hard rules you must answer to. This is *your* creative work.

Asking yourself the previous questions is just a powerful way to look at your book to determine how easily a potential reader will be attracted to it—and buy it.

## CHAPTER 2 – Goal, motivation, and conflict

Every story—no matter the genre—must contain the essential elements of good story-telling.

Characters have goals they are motivated to accomplish.

Their motivations fall into one or more of three categories:
- money
- love
- revenge

That's it.

With no conflict, there is no story.

Who wants to read a story about a guy who got up in the morning, shaved, took the bus to work, came home, ate dinner, watched TV and went to bed?

Conflicts happen that question the outcome of a story.

Conflict has also been referred to as "the hero's journey." The story of the hero on a quest, facing danger and adversity along the way, is timeless.

There are three different kinds of conflict:
- inner conflict,
- personal conflict between people, and
- universal conflict, that is, conflict between you and everyone else.

Does your story contain one—or more—of these three kinds of conflict?

New York literary agent Donald Maass, who wrote *Writing the Breakout Novel*, describes conflict as, "Someone wants something, and there's an obstacle."

In one of his workshops that I attended he emphasized that he wants to see "conflict on every page." He said, "It's the single most important thing you can do to take your novel to break-out level."

The obstacle in your conflict can be as simple as your protagonist looks forward to dining in his favorite restaurant and finds it closed, or as complicated as your protagonist having to choose between saving the life of his mother or the life of his child.

In your story, are the hero's goal, motivation, and the conflict he faces clear?

Great conflict can happen when two of your main characters want opposite things. They both can't win. Will one win, or will there be a compromise?

If you want to know more about this subject and the story parts I'm going to tell you about in the next chapter, I highly recommend *Story*, by Robert McKee. This book should be on every fiction writer's bookshelf.

## CHAPTER 3 – The parts of your novel, and what they should do

### The STORY part of your story

**Stories** are often referred to as being told in three acts, or three parts. This story-telling "formula" dates way back to the times of Greek tragedies and comedies. You may hear other writers refer to "the story arc." Basically, this is the same thing.

Just like doctors and mechanics, we writers love our own special vocabulary!

Broken down, here is a rough idea of story acts or how a story arc unfolds:

**Part One/Act One**—whatever you want to call it, is the beginning of the book.

This is where something happens that creates a story. This "something happening" is called "the INCITING INCIDENT." This means that whatever happens in the beginning of your story is going to cause all the actions and feelings and scenes that follow.

Ideally, the inciting incident will change the life of your character forever after.

What is the inciting incident in your story?

Does it begin on the first page so that the reader is immediately drawn in? Generally the inciting incident is some kind of action, something the main character must *immediately* react to.

This hooks your reader into your story. Your reader is already wondering, who is this character? Why is he in this situation? How did this happen? OMG, what's he going to do?

Your reader keeps reading because he wants to know more about the character and the situation you've introduced.

In this first part you will also establish who your main characters are and what your story is about. Your reader will understand their relationships and the world they live in. Your reader also will understand the values at stake for the characters.

**Part Two/Act Two** presents a culminating crisis or a confrontation.

The conflict resulting from the inciting incident builds. Your protagonist may use different ways to solve the challenge, none of which work. This can be the blackest moment for your character. The moment when it seems all hope is lost.

OMG, what will he do *now*?

**Part Three/Act Three** presents the resolution. The journey or quest ends, not surprisingly, with the conflict being resolved. This usually happens in a climactic scene where all the actions in the story come to a head. Often it is intense and dramatic and resolves the conflicts for the protagonist and other characters.

The idea here is that every great story has a clear beginning, middle, and end—three parts. That is not to say that they will be necessarily three *equal* parts. The beginning, for example, may be much longer than the middle and the end.

Does your novel have a clear story structure?

Can you define the beginning, middle and end?

Steve Windsor, in his ebook *Nine Day Novel Writing*, does a great job of explaining story structure in a way that's quick and easy to understand.

And of course, Robert McKee addresses this in great detail in *Story*, that much bigger, thicker book.

**The DESCRIPTION part of your story**

Descriptions tied to emotions, telling us how the character FEELS about something, are the most powerful.

In my eco-adventure romance, *Hard Amazon Rain*, a tarantula has become entangled in the hair of my protagonist:

*"Get it out. Ohhh... get it out." Dianti shuddered and swayed. Tears stung her eyes. She spread her hands flat on the ground to keep herself steady. She tried to focus on—a stone on the ground? Yes, the doctor said at times of stress to focus on an object.*

Donald Maas says, "It's the details that you remember, that trigger the emotion."

Ask yourself: Does the description remind your character of something else? Perhaps something personal? You want to write details that evoke emotion and present vivid imagery.

Descriptions are strongest when seen from the point of view of the dominant character in the scene. We're going to talk about this point of view concept a little further on.

The purpose of describing something is to set the scene or illustrate. It must support the story. Look at your descriptive words to see if there is any way you can strengthen them by being more specific.

For instance:

animal = cat = ocelot

dress = house dress = shirtwaist

purse = handbag = Gucci

Descriptions can be a little longer in scenes that are more reflective or are backstory.

In action scenes, you want to keep your descriptions as short and clear as possible. You want to keep the action moving, not slow the pacing with a lengthy description of the parts of the car that went end over end when it hit an embankment in the middle of the chase scene.

## The DIALOGUE parts of your story

Dialogue can do so many things that make your story powerful. It can

- show quirks of the speaking character
- comment on or establish the setting
- build conflict by providing drama
- foreshadow events to come
- give information and/or explain
- show emotion
- move the story forward

Dialogue is most effective when it is simple and emotionally charged.

Read your dialogue and ask yourself:
- Does what the character say make a point?
- Does the character speak simply? Most of us don't speak in complete sentences.
- How much emotion is in the words?

Be careful with characters who speak with dialects, accents or unusual speech mannerisms. Keep these examples to a minimum because this can be hard to read and can also slow pacing.

How does your dialogue *flow*?

What does that mean?

A good way to test for the "feel" of dialogue that is natural and flows well is to read it out loud. If you have written a long sentence for your character that you can't say out loud without taking a breath in the middle, that sentence is too long.

To learn more about dialogue, **study movie scripts**.

Look especially at action scenes that have dialogue.

Notice how few words are in each character's part. Notice the back and forth exchange of conversation.

Then look at tense, emotional scenes. Notice what words are used to convey meaning. Notice how the characters express their emotions in words.

You can download the complete scripts of many popular movies at www.simplyscripts.com. But beware—you could get hooked, like I did, on reading scripts of your favorite movies!

### The SCENES in your story

The function of a scene is to bring change—small or large—into the life of the character through an event.

This is really important. Let me repeat that.

*The function of a scene is to bring change—small or large—into the life of the character through an event.*

Now, when I say "event" I don't necessarily mean major action.

The *event* in the scene could be as simple as your character looks out the kitchen window at the neighbor's yard, has an epiphany, and *makes a decision* to divorce her husband. That decision *will bring change* into her life.

The conflict within a scene will present a cause and effect dynamic that can take your character from one emotion to another.

Is your first—and most important—scene an INCITING INCIDENT?

Remember, this is the setup for your entire story, the incident that introduces your character and at least hints at conflict to come. **This event must raise questions.** Otherwise your characters have no story goal, and your reader has no reason to keep reading.

From this beginning on, your character must make choices that move the story forward.

Is there **TENSION** in your scene?

Escalating tension keeps your reader engaged in your story, making for an exciting, can't-put-the-book-down read.

Ask yourself these important questions about each scene in your manuscript:

- What is the point of this scene?
- Does the reader know immediately where and when this scene takes place?
- What is at stake in this scene?
- What does this scene reveal?
- How does this scene move the story forward?
- Is this scene an interesting event?
- Does the scene end hinting at something that will make the reader want to continue reading? A large—or small—cliffhanger?
- What has changed for the character from the beginning of the scene to the end of the scene?
- If I eliminated this scene, would it hurt the story? This

question helps you know how important this scene is to the story.

There is no average scene word count. The scene can be as short or as long as it takes to do what it needs to do.

**The POINT OF VIEW parts of your story**
Remember earlier I mentioned POINT OF VIEW?
In your writing, POINT OF VIEW (POV) is something you need to be clear about.

In considering POV, you want to ask yourself in each scene, who is experiencing this? Usually this will be the main character in the scene.

Everything seen, heard, tasted, thought and felt is done by this character.

If you attribute any of these things to other persons in the scene, you are doing what is called "head-hopping." (More writer-speak vocabulary!)

The main reason you don't want to head-hop is that it confuses the reader. It makes it harder for the reader to identify with and care about what's happening to a key character, and if they don't care, they won't continue to read your story.

If your story is told in FIRST PERSON, then the point of view is always going to be yours as the writer. Everything seen, imagined, questioned or noticed is by YOU.

For instance, from this point of view you can't write, *"My sister thought he was really an evil man."* You CAN write, *"My sister told me she thought he was really an evil man."*

Here are the four major points of view you want to be aware of:

**FIRST PERSON POV**
You are writing the story told from your point of view.

*I roll down the Cadillac's windows to enjoy the night desert's pungent sage smell. It will help to clear my drink- and drug-filled head. (Coming to Las Vegas)*

I have described my situation and the environment around me. It is clearly *my* impression.

All memoir is FIRST PERSON POV.

**OMNISCIENT or "all-knowing" POV**

Think of this like television news coverage, with reporters and cameras everywhere. They talk about what people are doing at the scene, what people are thinking, and speculate on what's going to happen.

When you write about a character, *"Little did she know that the following year she would be living in a different town",* that is OMNISCIENT POV.

I advise you to use it sparingly because it's not particularly a warm and fuzzy POV. It keeps the reader distanced so that it's harder for him to become emotionally involved.

OMNISCIENT POV is an outdated POV. Decades ago in fiction it was prevalent, but today readers want a faster-paced, tighter story, with clear focus. They want to be immediately engaged and emotionally involved with your main characters.

OMNISCIENT POV is also a difficult POV to write because it doesn't relate to the reader's experience of reality. He can't know everything that's going on elsewhere in the story and in the lives of the characters or in their future. He can't identify with this all-knowing approach in the story, either.

## A MINOR CHARACTER'S POV

Think of your neighbor telling you a story about a celebrity for whom he used to work. The story is about the celebrity, but the narrator is a minor character in that person's life.

The reader only gets to see what the minor character sees. The minor character cannot describe, for example, a bedroom scene with dialogue if he wasn't there.

The best example of this is *The Great Gatsby*, where the entire story of Jay Gatsby and Daisy Buchanan is told from the viewpoint of Nick Carraway, a man who lives on the peripheral of Jay and Daisy's world.

In today's popular fiction, we seldom see this technique.

## MULTIPLE POVs

When you have more than one POV, even if you have only two viewpoints, you have MULTIPLE POVs. This is not the same as omniscient POV. This simply means that the story is alternately told from the POV of more than one main character.

You'll find this common in modern fiction written in third person.

A rule of thumb is that a SCENE be told from just one character's POV. You want to strive throughout your story for a balance of character viewpoints in scenes and/or chapters if you are using multiple POVs.

In *The Poisonwood Bible*, Barbara Kingsolver does a brilliant job of writing in multiple first person POVs. Each woman has a chapter devoted to moving the story along, but told from her individual POV. This is all the more interesting because Kingsolver writes each chapter in FIRST PERSON POV, and each woman has her own distinctive "voice."

It's sometimes easy to switch POVs when you're writing without being aware that you are doing so. This "head-hopping" disturbs the reader's thought process and can confuse him.

When your scene is clearly in one character's POV, you can eliminate a lot of redundant words like *saw* and *felt* because it is clear to the reader who is seeing and feeling.

POV can become an issue when you are writing in third person, because each character may see the environment and action around him differently.

Another rule of thumb is that the scene will be strongest if the POV is from the character WHO HAS THE MOST AT STAKE.

James Patterson talks about this in his Master Class on novel writing, *James Patterson Teaches Writing*. He likes to write his novels in both first person and what he calls "limited third person" POVs.

He says that it's easier for him to get into the scene with first person. The limitation is that this is the only character you can follow.
Because he likes to follow the villains, too, he writes short, precise third person scenes also, usually focusing on the villain's thinking combined with some action.

Patterson advises that you ask yourself, "Whose POV makes this more interesting? What's going to make this come alive the best?"

If you want to know more about point of view, just Google it and you'll find numerous articles on how best to use it.

## CHAPTER 4 – About your characters...

Are your characters believable?

Are your characters memorable?

Great stories are CHARACTER-DRIVEN. Think Scarlet O'Hara, James Bond, Madame Bovary, Harry Potter, Sukie Stackhouse, Jack Bauer.

No one is all good, or all bad. MEMORABLE CHARACTERS have a small part of themselves that is opposite to their dominant beliefs and behaviors. Consider the cliché of the hooker with a "heart of gold", or the serial killer who sets a bowl of cream on his porch for a feral kitten.

Often memorable characters are also FLAWED characters. Nobody is perfect. Your character's flaw makes him more human, vulnerable, and easy for the reader to identify with and care about. It makes your character more believable.

And a BELIEVABLE character is one your reader will easily identify with and care about.

Now, your character may realize he has a certain peculiar trait, but not see it as a flaw.

For instance, he might see it as a way he protects himself from the rest of the world. But this flaw can hinder him in accomplishing his goal.

Hey, another opportunity for CONFLICT!

A flaw can be a strength taken too far. For instance, a heroine who is too trusting, a dedicated entrepreneur who becomes a workaholic, a cop who insists on doing everything by the book.

What is your character's greatest strength? How can that become a flaw that holds him back?

Your character's flaw can be emotional, intellectual, or even physical, like WWI veteran Richard Harrow in the TV series *Boardwalk Empire*.

Choose a flaw that will hinder him most in the challenging situation you've put him in.

Remember the scene in *Indiana Jones* where he looks down into the pit and exclaims, "Snakes! I *hate* snakes!"

Consider your story and for each character ask yourself:

>**Who** is my character?
>**What** does s/he want?
>**Why** does s/he want it?
>**How** does s/he go about getting it?
>**What** stops him/her?
>**What** will happen if s/he doesn't get it? What are the consequences?

Here's a fun exercise to help you think about how to make your character memorable:

Let's take Captain Jack Sparrow from the *Pirates of the Caribbean* movies. Think about him and ask yourself:

—What makes him so relatable and likeable?
—What is his biggest flaw?
—What are his memorable expressions?
—What are his memorable habitual physical movements?

You can also do this exercise by thinking about what actor or actress you would like to see playing the role of your main character(s). Then ask yourself the previous questions about that person.

Next I want you to ask yourself:

**Why** is my character doing this? Why now?
**What** does my character believe that motivates him/her to make this choice?

Does this sound like I'm talking again about GOAL, MOTIVATION & CONFLICT?

YES! You're getting it!

When you can answer these questions, you most likely have a STRONG, BELIEVABLE and MEMORABLE character with whom your reader can identify.

You want your character to come across as intelligent in his or her own way. You don't want what romance readers call "a heroine who is too stupid to live."

Next we're going to talk about your characters in their relation to the PLOT POINTS in your story.

## CHAPTER 5 – Your story's plot points

Do the PLOT POINTS (more writer-speak) in your story make sense?

The last thing you want is for your reader to throw your book down in disgust and declare, "That is so stupid! That would never happen!"

How many times have you heard or read that if you come home and find your door ajar, you should NOT ENTER, but immediately leave and call the police?

Yet in so many television dramas I see the main character walk right in—albeit with caution—while in my head I'm screaming, "That's STUPID! Don't do that!" To me, that is cliché action and borderline "would never happen."

Even if you write sci-fi or horror, actions in your story must make sense. It is this sense of "normal" that pulls your reader in emotionally. Stephen King is a master of this.

Look at each event in your story and ask yourself: Does it make sense that after "this" happened, my character does "that"?

Think of the concept of CAUSE AND EFFECT. For every action there is a reaction. For example, the inciting incident is the *cause* that affects the rest of the story.

Does your character's BACK STORY (there's that writer-speak again) support their decision to react in a certain way? Does it make sense that given who he is, your character would make this decision?

A good way to get a handle on this is to create a separate document from your story and call it, "Timeline." This will help you establish what happens after each action and will help you to be clear in telling that to your reader.

A Timeline will help you with your story details as well. You don't want your character to travel in Los Angeles from point A to point B in 5 minutes where your reader knows it really takes 2 hours in normal traffic.

CHARTING OUT THE PLOT POINTS IN A TIMELINE is the best way I've found to make sure everything makes sense.

## CHAPTER 6 – The power of the five senses

Have you taken full advantage of the power of THE FIVE SENSES?

- What does your character **SEE**? What does it mean to him/her? How does it make your character FEEL?

- What does your character **HEAR**? What does it mean to him/her? How does it make your character FEEL?

- What can your character **TOUCH**? What does it mean to him/her? How does it make your character FEEL?

- What does your character **SMELL**? What does it mean to him/her? How does it make your character FEEL?

- What does your character **TASTE**? What does it mean to him/her? How does it make your character FEEL?

Notice how for each sense I asked you to relate it to how your character FEELS. It's that thing about EMOTION, again.

Here is an overview of how you might USE THE SENSES TO POWER UP your story-telling:

### SIGHT

Of the five senses, sight has been proven by psychologists to be the dominant one for normal people. As writers, it's the one we rely on most heavily—sometimes too heavily.

Here's the order in which we see things:

1. Spatial dimension – how big, how wide, how high, how far is it?

2. Source of light  – is it light or dark? Natural or artificial? Where does the light come from?

3. Dominant colors – Is the room decorated in garish reds? Is it dusk, when the natural colors of the rainbow fade into neutrals of gray? Is she wearing your favorite shade of blue?

4. Texture – Does it look rough like granite boulders? Smooth like slotted cream? Furry like a newborn kitten?

5. Contrasting shades – what in the room stands out in the light and what is obscured in shadow?

## HEARING

Hearing is the second thing we immediately notice.

1. Loudness  – is the sound blaring? Or is it so quiet as to be almost indistinguishable?

2. Tonality – Is it harsh? Strident? Soft? Melodious?

3. Source  – Where is the sound coming from? Above? Outside? Next door? Far away? The corner of the room?

4. Identity – is it easy or difficult to identify where the sound is coming from? Is the sound familiar? Does it sound like it could be...? What?

5. Interpretation of the sound – does it make you feel like you are back at a high school dance? Does it make goosebumps rise on your arms? Does it remind you of a past event? Here we go again with those EMOTIONS and FEELINGS …

**SMELL**

Smell ranks third in the list and comes far below sight and hearing because it is the most primitive sense and one we often notice last.

SMELL is the sense most often overlooked by writers. Yet it can make a scene come to life in your reader's mind because this is the sense that will EVOKE MEMORY FASTER than any other.

Strong odors are noticed more often. We process them to decide if we find them to be pleasant or unpleasant.

**TOUCH**

Touch is a sense we, as writers, are conscious of to a large degree.

Certainly ROMANCES are very physical, intimate stories where touch plays an important role in their telling. In THRILLERS and SUSPENSE, touch can also play a major role.

While TOUCH is usually the one sense we seldom overlook, when we do, the story lacks not only in the feel of the telling, but also strength in the plot itself.

Consider then:

1. The smoothness of wet skin

2. The sensuality of material on naked flesh

3. The roughness of a calloused hand

4. The silkiness of hair

5. The vibration of a cat's purr

6. The coldness of a snowball

**TASTE**

In writing, taste is the least used of all the senses.

Since taste usually entails food or putting something in the mouth, unless your characters romp through your manuscript pages from one meal to another, there may not be a lot of places where you can use it.

However, when your character puts something in his/her mouth, transmit the experience to your reader.

Is the taste salty? Sweet? Coarse? Smooth? Bitter? Hot? Cold? Lukewarm? Icy?

**Not all of THE FIVE SENSES will be appropriate in every scene.** But I want you to be aware of how powerful the five senses can be in creating a story your reader can visualize and identify with.

If you can use at least two or three of them, your scene will have more POWER.

And MORE POWER is why you're reading this book,

right?

## CHAPTER 7 – Developmental/content editing vs. copy/line editing

Remember in the introduction to this book I told you there are two kinds of editors you can hire?

The first kind of editing involves looking at your story itself. This has been the major focus of Part One of this book.

A Developmental or Content Editor—really the same thing—will critique and evaluate your story based on all the things I told you about in Chapters 1 through 6.

S/he, looking at the big picture, will look for inconsistencies in your story-telling and may suggest possible revisions that will make your story move forward with smoother pacing.

A Copy or Line Editor reads every line with a focused eye on words that are misspelled, names that are inconsistently spelled, punctuation, typos, and glaring grammar errors.

## CHAPTER 8 – Three key critiques for your story

Whew!

So far I've given you a lot to think about. I hope you're not in overwhelm.

Need a fresh cup of coffee? Because we have a lot more to cover in PART TWO before you're done with this POWER EDIT of your manuscript.

Meanwhile here are THREE KEY CRITIQUES for your story.

Why not write these out on a big sheet of paper and tape it to the wall you look at while you're writing?

### 1— IS MY MAIN CHARACTER MEMORABLE?

Why?

Can I add a special trait to make him/her more memorable?

If you need to review, it was CHAPTER 4 where I talked about making your characters memorable and believable.

### 2— WHAT COULD ENHANCE EMOTION?

Could I find a more powerful word or phrase?

Can I add more nonverbal communication?

You may want to review CHAPTER 6 where I talked about using the five senses.

### 3— HOW CAN I UP THE STAKES?

Why does anyone (your reader) care about what's in this line or on this page?

What challenge/setback could I add that would make the problem count more?

Can I add an unexpected complication?

You may want to review CHAPTER 2 on Goal, Motivation and Conflict.

Could a character's goal be bigger? Could his or her motivation be stronger? Could the conflict be heightened to be edgier, darker .... ?

Okay, now onto the more gritty details of POWER EDITING.

# PART TWO: YOUR WRITING

### CHAPTER 9 – Five edit "searches" that will strengthen your writing

The computer is my candidate for the eighth wonder of the world.

When a friend of mine told me he wrote his entire book in long-hand, I was stunned. What a tedious, time-consuming feat, I thought. I've been typing since high school and can't imagine any other way to write anything beyond a haiku or single-sentence journal entry.

To me, the real POWERS of our modern writing tool, the computer, are SPELL-CHECK and WORD COUNT and their sister, EDIT/FIND.

With EDIT/FIND I can search only for words that slow down the flow and readability of my writing and kick out a lot of them.

I've identified FIVE WORDS that consistently fall into this category.

Here's how I use EDIT/FIND to "weed" my writing after the first or second draft:

1. In my Word program, I select EDIT from the tool bar,

then scroll down and click on FIND. In the search box, usually found in the upper left hand corner of your word document, I type only two letters: *ly.*

Up will pop words like quickly, immediately, suddenly, warmly, quietly, softly, instantly, darkly, etc. I examine carefully each sentence where an *ly* word pops up.

For example, in the previous sentence, could I have written *with care* rather than *carefully? With care* is only two syllables and when read out loud sounds stronger.

**Among other reasons, I like to read my sentences out loud to imagine how they might sound if my novel ever became an audio book.**

2. The next edit/find I do is for the word *very.*

What is the difference between a night that is dark and a night that is *very* dark?

The only thing *very* does here is slow pacing and add to your word count. Out it goes.

3. The word ***and*** is another edit/find. Often you'll find that two simple sentences can be more powerful than one compound sentence using *and*.

4. ***Then*** is a word to watch out for. You want to avoid any sentence that reads like *"Then she did this and then she did that. Then she went there…"*

Another example: *"He lit the match and then the building exploded"* is not as powerful as, *"He lit the match and the building exploded."*

5. *That* often is not a necessary word in a sentence, especially if it's dialogue.

When my character speaks, most likely his grammar is not perfect. He'd be more likely to say *"I hated that dress she wore"*, rather than *"I hated that dress that she wore."*

Often, you'll find you can eliminate *that* from a sentence and it will flow much better.

I'm not saying these words should be completely eliminated from your work. It's just that we tend to overuse them.

By examining each use you can determine where a substitute phrase or elimination will strengthen a sentence, and in turn strengthen your story-telling.

I continue to select "find next" until I've searched my entire manuscript for these words and determined where it is appropriate to keep them and where they may changed or eliminated.

## CHAPTER 10 – A powerful, magical editing system

I want to introduce you to Margie Lawson.

Several years ago I took Margie's Deep Editing workshop online. It *absolutely and immediately* added the POWER that took my writing to a higher level.

And that's what you want.

You want to edit your book in a way that will take it to a higher, more powerful level. A way that will make it impact your reader in a MEMORABLE way.

So who is Margie Lawson and why am I such a big fan?

Margie Lawson holds a Master of Science degree in Counseling Psychology with an additional two-year post-masters specialization in psychiatric counseling and marriage and family therapy.

So wouldn't you think she knows a lot about MOTIVATION and EMOTION?

Margie says, "I am fascinated with the emotive power of words. How can writers 'up' the emotive power of their work? By tuning in to the nuances of their characters' nonverbal communication. By writing visceral emotion and body language to strengthen subconscious connections with the reader. By editing deep…to capture the perfect balance of dialogue, visceral emotion, body language, action, setting, internalizations, and tension for each scene. The goal is to entrance the reader, lead them into your fictional world, and make them beg to stay."

Yes!

Towards this end, she has created a system that applies to writing fiction what she knows about human psychology.

Using Margie Lawson's HIGHLIGHTING SYSTEM, you can look at the balance of what you have in each scene and on each page.

The following is an introduction to Margie Lawson's EDITS System. For the complete, in-depth application of this powerful editing tool, go to www.margielawson.com.

For this exercise you are going to need different colored HIGHLIGHTERS: Pink, blue, yellow, orange and green.

Plus a red pen.

Need more coffee?

Here we go.

### E = EMOTION
With a PINK highlighter, mark any words and phrases that describe a physical representation of emotion. Emotions are usually expressed in internalizations, dialogue, some actions, and nonverbal communication.

What you want to highlight with PINK, is the INVOLUNTARY PHYSICAL RESPONSE TO

EMOTION. To find this you must look for words that describe a physical response.

For example, a blush is involuntary, so it's PINK. So would be the stomach lurching, sweat forming on the brow, the heart pounding.

Where you have PINK, you know this is where the reader will be emotionally hooked.

### D = DIALOGUE
With a BLUE highlighter, mark just the dialogue, just what's INSIDE the quotation marks.

That's easy, right?

### I = INTERNALIZATIONS
With a YELLOW highlighter, mark everything the POV character is thinking (internalization), including exposition and backstory.

Some authors put **internalizations**—the character's thoughts—in italics. The trend now seems to be to leave them in regular type, unless it's a single word or short phrase that you might want to italicize for emphasis.

**Exposition** is sharing straight factual information.

**Backstory** is any reference you make to events of the character's past.

While you do need YELLOW, you don't want to have big sections of yellow.

### T = TENSION/CONFLICT

With an ORANGE highlighter, you want to track TENSION and CONFLICT.

Track this in the margins of your page, because it may overlap other colors in the text.

You might have a long line of ORANGE all down the side of a page.

That's great!

## S = SETTING/DESCRIPTION
With a GREEN highlighter, mark words and phrases that indicate SETTING, as well as the PHYSICAL FEATURES of a character, including what they are wearing.

I told you this would be easy!

## RED UNDERLINE
Underline any PHYSICAL ACTION or MOVEMENTS in red.

Actions and movements can include facial expressions, gestures, nods, walking, sitting, turning, leaning—as well as any nonverbal communication such as stares, looks or glances.

## NOW TURN YOUR PAGE UPSIDE DOWN!

Margie suggests that you turn your page upside down and look at those highlighted lines.

Ask yourself:
1) What are the predominate colors on which pages?
2) What colors are barely present?

3)  Do you have any long passages of dialogue (BLUE) that render more white space on the page(s)?
4)  Is there a big patch of YELLOW? Staying too long inside a character's head?

**Watch out!**  Fiction readers today want to get right to the heart of the story, right into the action and the dialogue.

Be aware that if you have several lines or paragraphs of green or yellow, your reader will tend to skim these long sections of description and internalizations.

Margie says, "BLUE and RED make for a FAST READ."

John Locke's e-books are a good example of this. Stuart Woods' books are also heavy on action and dialogue. James Patterson, who, according to Nielsen BookScan, has sold more books in the past decade than any other writer, is the master of the fast, exciting read.

## CHAPTER 11 – Those boring, tiresome clichés

I hate how many times I heard this in high school English class. Now I have to admit the teacher was right.

DON'T WRITE WITH CLICHÉS!

Okay, I know all caps indicate yelling. But the teacher yelled at me, so now I get to yell at you.

Certain phrases (two or more words) have become so overused that the expression is no longer either clever or novel. Now they're just boring and tiresome. They no longer have any strength of meaning. They don't add any specific details that give the reader a clear picture with which to identify.

They are so generalized they contribute *nothing* to the story you are writing.

Theodore Rees Chaney addressed clichés in *GETTING THE WORDS RIGHT: How to Revise, Edit and Rewrite.* While he wrote this book in 1984 and revised it in 1990, his advice remains sound.

To help you find places in your manuscript where you may have inadvertently used a cliché, run an EDIT/FIND for the words *like* and *as.* These two words often precede a cliché.

Here are some common clichés to search for:

Acid test
Bad blood
Bated breath
Beat a hasty retreat
Bit off more than he could chew
Boggles the mind
Bound and determined
By the same token
Can of worms
Dull thud
End of her rope
End result
Fell swoop
Green with envy
Half the battle
Hit the sack
Lead balloon
Lion's share
Lock, stock and barrel
Name of the game
Nick of time
Over a barrel
Sick and tired
Sickening thud
Tail between his legs
Ton of bricks
Toss and turn
Ulterior motive
Vast wasteland
Vicious circle

This is NOT to be considered a complete list. There are many more clichés you'll hear every day.

A great website that lists the largest collection of clichés ever compiled is www.clichesite.com.
On this site you can search for clichés alphabetically by the first word of the cliché phrase, submit a cliché if you don't see it listed, and even check on their "Cliché of the Day."

*Writers' Digest* has published a list of 12 clichés for all writers to avoid. To find out what they are, go here: www.writersdigest.com/online-editor/12-cliches-all-writers-should-avoid

Googling *cliché* will bring up a long list of sites where you can explore this subject further.

The one place you might consider using a cliché in your writing is in DIALOGUE. For example, speaking in clichés might be one character's particular trait.

Because I wrote my memoir, *Coming to Las Vegas,* in first person, present tense, and part of what I wanted to convey was my "young" voice, I felt okay writing:
*Lara prays Alice will get her act together, and soon.*

And here's how I used a cliché in dialogue:
*"Poor Donald was a nervous wreck the whole time we were there."*

Now, having told you NOT to use clichés, I want to share with you how to TWEAK a cliché to make it work in a creative way for you.

When you find a cliché in your manuscript, don't dump it immediately just because it's a cliché. There may be a way to tweak it so that it becomes a clever use of descriptive words.

Let's take "bad blood" for example. Instead of writing, *There was bad blood between them,* you could write, *Between them was the baddest blood in the county.*

In my novel, *IMPLOSION,* instead of "green with envy", I wrote: *Every other journalist in the city room, including her nemesis, Mike Mabbett, was chartreuse with envy.*

And, instead of "mind their own business", I wrote this in dialogue: *"Yeah, well, everybody should mind their own assignments."*

And, instead of "song-and-dance", I wrote: *The show opened with the expected song-and-prance numbers.*

And, instead of "love at first sight", I wrote: *It had been lust at first sight.*

In my Las Vegas memoir I took the cliché "making money hand over fist" and wrote: *They're making money hand over greedy fist.*

In *Magicide,* instead of saying "too close to home", I wrote: *She had to trust that in their interview Larissa wouldn't reveal anything too close to Cheri's home.*

And in *Magicide,* for the cliché "dressed to kill", I wrote: *Cheri was surrounded by attendees, all dressed to thrill.*

By now, I'm sure you get the picture.

You are a creative writer telling a unique story. You don't need the same overused, every day clichés.

## CHAPTER 12 – Tautologies – a big no no

Tautologies are redundancies. When you use two words in a phrase, technically you now have said the same thing twice.

For example, *baby puppies*. By definition, puppies are babies. The word "baby" is therefore redundant.

Here's a short list of what could be a list of thousands of tautologies:

Bare naked
Basic fundamentals
Burn down
Burning hot
Cancel out
Climb up
Close proximity
Completely destroyed
Conversational dialogue
Definite decision
Disorganized mess
First priority
Foreign import
Free gift
Frigid ice
Honest truth
Kneel down
Morning sunrise
New innovation
New recruit

Protrude out
Recur again
Reiterate again
Retreat back
Sad misfortune
Shared dialogue
Stand up
Sit down
Short midget
Short summary
Tall giant
Three-sided triangle
Totally unanimous
Two-way dialogue
Unsolved mystery
Vast majority

*STAND UP, SIT DOWN*, and *CLIMB UP* are tautologies? Yes. We're so accustomed to hearing those phrases that we often automatically type them. If you've used them in your manuscript, an Edit/Find for the word "up" will find them.

Are you still with me?

Because next we are going to look at some powerful writing tools called RHETORICAL DEVICES.

## CHAPTER 13 – The power of rhetorical devices

What are rhetorical devices?

According to the dictionary, a RHETORICAL DEVICE is a use of language that creates a literary effect—but often without regard for literal significance.

On her website, www.margielawson.com, Margie Lawson lists over thirty rhetorical devices! One more reason you should check out this woman's awesome information.

Following are the ones that I think are the most powerful and easy to incorporate into your writing. You can use them right now to power-up your sentences and paragraphs.

### CAROLYN'S FAVORITE
### 12 POWERFUL RHETORICAL DEVICES

**1) ALLITERATION** – This happens when you REPEAT INITIAL CONSONANT SOUNDS.

Remember "Peter Piper picked a peck of pickled peppers"?

Words with initial consonant sounds may be juxtaposed, next to each other, or they may be spread out in one sentence or across several sentences.

*"Let some other detective investigate the **sins of Sin City** tonight." (Magicide)*

*He had a **finger flint flasher** and ball of **flash** cotton stashed in his pocket. (Magicide)*

**2) ANADIPLOSIS** – This is when you REPEAT THE LAST WORD OR PHRASE of one sentence at the beginning of the next sentence.

*As we enter the casino Del smiles and tells me about the Chairman of the board Bill **Bennett**. "**Bennett** hates that pink, but his business instinct can't argue with its success." (Coming to Las Vegas)*

My friend, comedian Jeff Wayne, is currently writing a memoir about his son who was diagnosed at age sixteen with schizoaffective disorder and ultimately killed himself at twenty-eight. Here's how Jeff used anadiplosis for emphasis:
*When the rush was on there would **be a lot of pressure. A lot of pressure** meant a lot of stress and stress was the one thing that he had to avoid.*

**3) ANAPHORA** – (the accent is on the second syl-LA-ble) – This is when you REPEAT A WORD OR PHRASE at the beginning of three (or four) successive phrases or sentences.

The first three are always in a row.

***They hated** it every time this man grabbed their asses. **They hated** it every time this man said something lewd under his* *breath as they passed by. **They hated** this man with a vengeance. (Coming to Las Vegas)*

Jeff Wayne uses ANAPHORA here:
***There were days when** it was tough to reach him. **There were days when** it was tough to get him to do his chores. **There were days when** Aaron would get up and get all his chores done and be full of energy.*

The above passage is stronger emotionally than it would have been if he had written:
*There were days when it was tough to reach him and to get him to do his chores, but some days Aaron would get up and get all his chores done and be full of energy.*

While three is strong, two can also have a significant effect.

***All of them** were magicians. **All of them** would know how to switch jump cuffs. (Magicide)*

***Three** is sometimes considered a lucky number. **Three** guarantees the ending would be exactly as he'd choreographed it. (Magicide)*

Margie Lawson says, "It's the rhythm. The echo. The repetition of the message." That's what makes ANAPHORA so powerful.

You can use ANAPHORA any time you want to emphasize a point, emphasize a thought, emphasize a feeling.

See what I just did in that last sentence?
**4) EPISTROPHE** – This is the counterpart to anaphora. WHEN YOU REPEAT THE LAST WORD or final

phrase in three (or four) subsequent phrases or sentences.

*What is it about this business that breeds **such conflict, such jealousy, such malice**? (Coming to Las Vegas)*

Here's how EPISTROPHE could be used in dialogue:
*"You want to keep sleeping with her, **then this relationship is over**. You want the world to answer to you, **then this relationship is over**. You want to forget you have kids, **then this relationship is over**."*

Pretty emphatic, huh? It's clear that this woman is not fooling around. It's also a good example of combining ANAPHORA **and** EPISTROPHE for greater impact.

Here's another example:
*"Nobody thinks **about it**, nobody cares **about it**, nobody does anything **about it**."*

The above example also combines ANAPHORA and EPISTROPHE. See how the word, *nobody* is repeated at the beginning of each phrase, and *about it* is repeated at the end of the phrase?

**5) ASYNDETON** – This happens when you OMIT CONJUNCTIONS between words and phrases in a list of three or more.

*It was Maxwell, chanting words about cleansing, renewal, rebirth, power, greatness. (Magicide)*

ASYNDETON can be used with equal effect with two words or phrases.

*She saw Tom off balance, his feet stumbling on the scarred wooden floor, his weight held by the older man's controlling hold. (Magicide)*

*You feel like anything is possible here—**the big score, the instant fame**. (Coming to Las Vegas)*

I could have written
*You feel like anything is possible here—the big score or instant fame.*

It's a subtle difference. Dropping the conjunction adds to the sense of tension.

Using asyndeton also picks up pace. It's direct and it sounds more spontaneous.

**6) EPIZEUXIS –** This is the repetition of a word or phrase for emphasis.

*She could **never** relax, **never** feel at home in a place like this. (Magicide)*

*The media blitz for the roller coaster escape had been enormous—**all people talked about** for weeks. Now **all people talked about** was his spectacular death. (Magicide)*

*"Robert the Great will perform the most dangerous **illusion** in the world. An **illusion** that has resulted in the death of at least twenty-three magicians in the history of all who have attempted it." (Magicide)*

*"**Never—never—never** let a bartender see you cry." (Coming to Las Vegas)*

Don't ask me how to pronounce EPIZEUXIS. I can't even tell from the dictionary.

**7) POLYSYNDETON** – This is when you use a conjunction (usually AND or OR) between a series of words in a list of three or more.

*She punched the numbers for Tom's cell and waited while it rang **and** rang **and** rang. (Magicide)*

*This was evidenced by the sniffles **and** wails **and** weeping when the service began. (Magicide)*

POLYSYNDETON can also be powerful and effective in non-fiction.

In her National Bestseller, *Bossypants*, Tina Fey writes: *There are hugs **and** kisses **and** pies **and** soup **and** ham **and** biscuits **and** a continuous flow of Maxwell House coffee with non-dairy creamer.*

And
*After a big family meal they rinse **and** scrape **and** dry **and** Saran-wrap like nobody's business.*

Here is another example from *"A" Is For Alibi* by Sue Grafton:
*There was really nothing open **or** loose **or** free about him….*

**8) LITOTE** – This is a form of UNDERSTATEMENT where an affirmative is expressed by the negative of its contrary. It generally uses the word, *not*.

Here are three examples from *IMPLOSION*:

*He'd thought of not bringing up the subject at all, but damned if he would let it go.*

*Not that she expected him to say anything profound, but maybe she could get lucky and spice up her review of the show with a quote from him.*

*Candy smiled, not really surprised at where this conversation appeared to be going.*

**9) EPONYM** – This is when you REFER TO A FAMOUS PERSON WHO IS RECOGNIZED FOR AN ATTRIBUTE and substitute their name for that attribute—but not necessarily mentioning the attribute—as in, *"She's a real Einstein."*

*Days go by with no action in Baccarat, and I can understand how **"Sophia Loren"** could become crazed with boredom. (Coming to Las Vegas)*

*Lara notices all the women are blondes and all the men dark and "**mafioso**-looking." (Coming to Las Vegas)*

*Donald wears black, horn-rimmed, **Clark Kent** glasses, so they call him, "Superman." (Coming to Las Vegas)*

*Angelina-Jolie lips, Foxy thought. (Implosion)*

To avoid confusion, you want to make the reference to very well-known people or events.

Perusing your manuscript, what characters have traits like famous people? What actions could be compared to a famous major world event? Does the city in your sci-fi novel resemble a haunted Chernobyl?

**10) HYPERBOLE** – This is where you use a deliberate exaggeration.

We use hyperbole a *gazillion* times in our everyday lives. These exaggerations are so common in our speech that we don't take them literally or think too much about them.

In fiction writing, HYPERBOLE will have more impact if you use it in thoughts and dialogue. For instance, your character says, *"I was so embarrassed I could have died a thousand times."*

*Won't happen, she reassured herself. I'm sure he's hung a million hammocks. (Hard Amazon Rain)*

*The rain drummed a steady cadence for forty-five minutes, a million fingers tappety-tapping on the roof. (Hard Amazon Rain)*

*She drank in the hundreds of rich shades of green and the pungent smell of damp earth. (Hard Amazon Rain)*

*"I think everybody who's anybody in Vegas was there, plus a zillion tourists." (Magicide)*

You may also want to use HYPERBOLE if you are writing your story in first-person.

*I'm thinking there are probably hundreds of thousands of MGM lion logos displayed everywhere, even in the carpeting design. (Coming to Las Vegas)*

The danger of using hyperbole is that often it can sound clichéd. Margie Lawson advises you to use hyperbole with caution.

**11) METAPHOR** – This is when you compare two different things by asserting that one thing is the other or has properties of the other.

*After living my entire life so far in Seattle, Detroit, and Los Angeles, this is **like another planet.** (Coming to Las Vegas)*

*This is how I would imagine you would be treated if you were **mafia princesses.** (Coming to Las Vegas)*

*Who will vote for a political candidate who looks **like a 1920s snake oil salesman?** (Coming to Las Vegas)*

And here is a use of metaphor in dialogue:

*The girls at my table stare at them. One says, "Gee, in these hats they look **like little organ grinder monkeys."** (Coming to Las Vegas)*

*He'd practiced for this position so many times that he no longer had concern for the tingles that felt **like his blood ran reversed through his veins.** (Magicide)*

**12) ONOMATOPOEIA** – This is when you create or use WORDS THAT IMITATE THE SOUND the word describes.

I do remember this word from my high school creative writing class. Just being able to pronounce it made me feel super-educated: "On – oh – motto – peeya."

*A **shwap** as she slams the drawer shut punctuates her scream. (Coming to Las Vegas)*

*Remaining quiet, she wandered close to a group of squirrel monkeys **chittering** above her head in the canopy. (Hard Amazon Rain)*

*Far off in the distance howler monkeys proclaimed the edge of their feeding territory with a lengthy, hollow **hooooooooo**. (Hard Amazon Rain)*

*Cheri turned the chicken carcass over. It hit the cutting board with a resounding **swaap**. (Magicide)*

*The elevator stopped with a **ka-klunk**, the doors parted and Linda stepped out. (Implosion)*

*Foxy's breath made a **tchssss** sound as he sucked hard on his mint. (Implosion)*

\* \* \*

Those are my favorite 12 RHETORICAL DEVICES. Whew! What a lot of choices.

I'm sure you'll remember seeing these rhetorical devices used in the novels you've read. Now you have names for them.

Are you still with me?

Don't try to memorize all these RHETORICAL DEVICES. My intention in listing them is to make you aware of the power of particular word arrangements in writing.

I don't remember them teaching any of these—except for ONOMATOPOEIA—in my high school English or Creative Writing classes. The emphasis then was on how to craft a grammatically correct complete or compound sentence.

When one of my fellow students pointed out to our Creative Writing teacher that Ernest Hemingway—her favorite author—did not write with a lot of complete sentences, she said, "You have to know the rules before you can break them."

## CHAPTER 14 – How active is your voice?

Have you used **active versus passive** voice as much as possible?

What I'm talking about is the TENSE of the verbs you use.

This is really easy to remember: Verbs that end in "ing" are passive. The rest of them are "active."

Here is an example of ACTIVE VOICE:

*Tonight's triumph **would take** his career to a dazzling new height. (Magicide)*

It would have been PASSIVE VOICE if I had written:
*Tonight's triumph **was going to take** his career to a dazzling new height.*

I also wrote
*On this curve of the track, his feet **lay** higher than his head.*

rather than
*On this curve of the track, his feet **were laying** higher than his head.*

because this is a suspenseful scene where there is no place for passive writing.

*In a wrinkled camp shirt, smudged pants, and those funny sandals, her sensuality **torched** his senses. (Hard Amazon Rain)*

I could have written:

*His senses **were torched** by the sensuality of her wrinkled camp shirt, smudged pants and funny sandals.*

The reason you want to use ACTIVE VOICE instead of PASSIVE VOICE is that it is a simpler, more straightforward kind of speech. And your story is about things that *happen* to your character now, right? Not things that are happening to people all the time.

The ACTIVE VOICE is perfect for the action that you describe (not *are describing*) in your story. You can tell if your sentence is passive if your subject is not performing a direct action.

I'm not saying PASSIVE VOICE is wrong. I'm saying it doesn't have much place in a story about people who take action and do/accomplish/escape from something.

Now, you may want to stop here, open your manuscript, and do an Edit/Find for "ing."

See if there are some places where you could rearrange the sentence that contains the "ing" word to make the voice active and more powerful.

But don't forget to come back! There's still more to do.

## CHAPTER 15 – Those nettlesome numbers

There are particular styles for writing numerals and numbers in fiction.

Writing numerals and numbers in an accepted style makes the pacing of the read smooth.

And, of course, there are always exceptions. It's your choice as the writer how you want to write numbers. Whichever way you choose, you want to be consistent throughout your manuscript.

**Here are the most accepted style rules:**

FOR **NUMBERS FROM ZERO THROUGH ONE HUNDRED,** spell them out. *One, two, three…ninety-nine.* Everything over one hundred, use numerals.

*It would exit the tunnel 595.42 feet from him.*

Spell out **NUMBERS THAT BEGIN A SENTENCE:** *Seventy percent of what comes out of the earth goes to the frontier traders and entrepreneurs.*

**COMPOUND NUMBERS,** from twenty-one to ninety-nine, are always hyphenated. As I wrote in the previous sentence.

*It tumbled forty-five feet to the pavement and shattered into a wreckage of twisted wood and metal and the bodies of its six passengers.*

**FRACTIONS** are spelled out and hyphenated: *One-third to one-half of them lived.*

In **DIALOGUE**, you want to spell the numbers out in words. *"It's twelve-thirty," he said. "Time to go."* Or *"I'm going to find that hidden six million dollars!"*

For **DEGREES** and **PERCENTAGES**, use words in both dialogue and narrative.

*Unusual, for hundred-degree weather. (Magicide)*

*"Imagine the money you'll lose with your work force reduced by eighty percent." (Hard Amazon Rain)*

Don't abbreviate the words *hours, years, pounds, ounces, feet, inches, yards* or *meters.*

*The emcee pointed upwards to the concave arc of the track, forty-five feet above the stage and lowered his voice. (Hard Amazon Rain)*

*The first lift of the Heldorado Hypercoaster passed through the roof of the casino to drop through a tunnel at eighty-six miles per hour. (Hard Amazon Rain)*

An exception could be *miles per hour*, where you might use *mph* if you would be repeating that a lot in your narrative.

But in dialogue, your character would be more likely to say, *"Eighty miles an hour is pretty fast."*

There are no hyphens between **NUMBERS AND PERCENT:**

*"But we could advance you ten percent out of our own pockets." (Hard Amazon Rain)*

*"Africa, Asia, South America—have sixty percent of all Christians worldwide, you see." (Hard Amazon Rain)*

**WRITING THE TIME** has always been confusing for me. You, too?

You don't have to use a.m. and p.m. If you do, use numbers: *I get up precisely at 7:15 a.m. every morning.* Notice also that a.m. and p.m. are in lower case letters.

You can write a.m. or p.m. or am or pm or capitalize them, but whichever method you choose, you want to write it the same way throughout your manuscript. Personally, I would not capitalize them.

The exception to using numbers in time is in dialogue. *"I can't believe he called me at five-thirty in the morning."*

If you write the word, *o'clock*, be sure you spell out the number before it: *Call me after seven o'clock.*

There are several different ways to write dates: the fifth of May; May 5th, May 5. If you follow the date with the year, you would not use *th: May 5, 2015.* The except is in dialogue, where you would always write, *"May fifth is the Cinco de Mayo celebration."*

**DECADES** can be tricky because they can be written as either words or numbers.
*I love all the music of the sixties.*

*The era of the big bands spanned from the 1930s to the 1950s.*

*"Here tonight Robert the Great, the first magician in the twenty-first century to attempt it, will catch a real bullet fired directly at him from a real rifle." (Magicide)*

*Four minutes later, her fear manifested in the form of a green '87 Honda Accord that pulled up in front of the magic shop and parked. (Magicide)*

Or as I used in my subtitle for *Coming to Las Vegas: A true tale of sex, drugs and Sin City in the '70s.*

Notice there is no apostrophe between the year and the letter "s".

The exception would be if the year is possessive: *He drove a vintage 1930's car.*

Centuries are always spelled out: *The Roaring Twenties was in the twenty-first century.*

Always spell out numbers in DIALOGUE.

*"Don't forget the fifty million reasons why Larissa would kill him." (Magicide)*

*"Hot out there. Prob'ly a hundred, already." (Magicide)*

The exception would be if your character referred to a year or an address:

*"They break a magic wand over the casket of the dead magician. It originated at Houdini's funeral in 1926." (Magicide)*

*"Abel and Mollie Franklyn. 19032 Boulder Highway, Henderson." (Magicide)*

**HEIGHTS** can also be written several different ways.

*In a corner, in a cage as tall as Carter's six-foot frame, Cheri estimated at least a dozen white doves. (Magicide)*

*Edmund Meiner had a hot tip from his bookie, a woman named Honey Gold he liked because she was six feet tall and sported a consistent uniform of black leather. (Magicide)*

*She was taller than Cheri expected; at five-feet-ten she didn't often meet a taller woman. (Magicide)*

The year is almost always written in numerals:

*Dressed in jeans and a black Maxwell Tour 2006 tee shirt, the young man hovered above him. (Magicide)*

**DOLLAR AMOUNTS** are written as numerals if you are using the dollar sign but if you are rounding the number, you would use words.

*SAG extras paid $75 a day for the duration of timing rehearsal and event. (Magicide)*

If you are writing about **GUNS**, you always want to capitalize the name of the manufacturer, i.e. *Ruger*. The word caliber is spelled out. Use numbers as the manufacturer does: *Colt .38* or *.357 Magnum* (notice the period before 38 and 357)

Milimeter can be written as it is often abbreviated: *mm.*

In dialogue you can go either way: *30.6* or *thirty aught six*.

In general spell it out unless it would be cumbersome.

In fiction, you can almost always substitute words for numerals. If you are unsure, it's easy to just Google, "How to write numbers in fiction."

**Whichever style you choose, be consistent.**
If in chapter two you write "twenty-third floor" be sure that in chapter nineteen you do not write "23$^{rd}$ floor."

Fiction has its own writing style. Instead of abbreviations and symbols, fiction writers use words.

The general rule of thumb is: when in doubt, spell it out.

## CHAPTER 16 – Names of books, plays, publications, songs, movies & TV shows

How do you know when to put names of books, plays, publications, songs, movies or TV shows in underline, quotes or italics?

Book publishers usually follow the journalist's guide, *The Chicago Manual of Style*.

Here's the skinny according to *The Chicago Manual of Style*:

Whether they are in narrative or dialogue, titles of books, newspapers, magazines, plays, operas, podcasts and other freestanding works are italicized. So are album titles and titles of long pieces of music.

Ship names are also italicized.

The murky water, lapping at her hull, sparkled with the *Rio Vida's* bright yellow reflection. *(Hard Amazon Rain)*

Dianti shaded her eyes with one hand and from the deck of the *Que Huevos*, she spotted the trimaran. *(Hard Amazon Rain)*

But not train names. That is according to *The Chicago Manual of Style* but many authors now commonly italicize train names and it is considered acceptable.

Titles of articles, chapters, TV episodes, blog posts, most poems, and other shorter works are enclosed in quotation marks.

By the way, sound words—remember "On – oh – motto – peeya" in chapter 13?—are always italicized.

Absorbed in his magazine, Tom didn't look up. "*Mmmm.*"
"*Mmmm* yes, *mmmm* no, *mmmm* what?" (Magicide)

So are foreign words.

Rocardo saw where she stared and announced, "*Araña! Tarántula!*" (Hard Amazon Rain)

Song titles go inside double quotation marks, unless your character in dialogue speaks about a specific song title, in which case it goes inside single quotation marks.

## CHAPTER 17 – That pesky punctuation

Why do we have to have punctuation, anyway?

We need punctuation to clarify the meaning of sentences.

For example, the commas in *Woman, without her man, is nothing* emphasize the importance of men, whereas *Woman: without her, man is nothing* emphasizes the importance of women.

Here's another one that's more amusing: *What's in the road ahead? What's in the road? A head?*

Lynne Truss emphasizes the importance of commas in the title of her best-selling book, *Eats, Shoots & Leaves: The Zero Tolerance Approach to Punctuation.*

Are you old enough to remember the *Encyclopedia Britannica*? Well, in the olden days—before Google—it was the ultimate reference for just about everything.

*Encyclopedia Britannica* says PUNCTUATION is "the use of spacing, conventional signs, and certain typographical devices as aids to the understanding and correct reading, both silently and aloud, of handwritten and printed texts."

I couldn't have said it more formally myself.

**The rules of punctuation are constantly evolving.**

That said, writers need to be aware of the importance of accepted punctuation styles.

You do have choices. Some kinds of punctuation will identify your style. Just remember to be consistent throughout your manuscript.

### The Period –
The period is found in more places than just the end of a sentence.

In acronyms, you don't want to use a period after each individual letter. For example, write *IRS*, not *I.R.S* and *HMS Bounty*, not *H.M.S. Bounty*.

In names, you want to use a period after any middle initial(s).
*John F. Kennedy* and *Wijnand A.P. Van Tilburg*

Always place a period inside a quotation mark that ends a sentence.
*Over the top of the car she said, "Magic, huh? But that's what Maxwell does." (Magicide)*

### The Comma –
Commas are probably the most misunderstood of all punctuation marks.

Use a comma after an introductory prepositional or participial phrase.
*Along with his other features, the cleft in his chin immediately identified him to Cheri. (Magicide)*

*Since she'd been in Peru, she'd learned little happened on pre-appointed time. (Hard Amazon Rain)*

Use a comma after an introductory subordinate clause.
*That said, writers need to be aware of the importance of accepted punctuation styles.*

Use a comma after phrases that show contrast.
*Digbee often stayed late, for his second love after performing was the business of magic. (Magicide)*

Use a comma to set off a direct quotation. Notice that in the first of the following two sentences the comma is INSIDE the closing quotation mark:
*"I have a lot of cargo," she said, gesturing to the crates around her. (Hard Amazon Rain)*

In this sentence, notice that the comma following the words *she said* is OUTSIDE the second opening quotation mark:
*"If my show wasn't temporarily dark," she said, "you'd never have found me awake at this ungodly hour."*
*(Magicide)*

Use commas to prevent misunderstanding in a sentence.
Remember, *Woman, without her man, is nothing* and *Woman: without her, man is nothing.*

Use a comma between the day of the month and the year.
*I'm writing this on June 17, 2015.*

Use a comma to separate items in a series.
*"Mechanics, timing, weight factors, the effects of the weather on the steel of the tracks, human error." (Magicide)*

With the word "and", either comma placement in both *red, white, and blue* and *red, white and blue* is acceptable today. Just remember throughout your novel to be consistent in which of these styles you choose.

**The Apostrophe –**

The apostrophe serves four purposes:

To show possession:
*Tired of yelling to be heard over the chug of **the boat's engine**, both men were silent. (Hard Amazon Rain)*

To show contraction:
*"But then, **that's** the attraction of major illusions." (Magicide)*

To show part of a word is missing:
*Sin City in the **'70s** (Coming to Las Vegas)*

*"This time you cannot sweet talk me into **takin'** you." (Hard Amazon Rain)*

To show a quote inside a quote:
*"He told me he didn't want to see anybody before the show. He needed to **'prepare himself mentally.'** But that's why I wanted to see him." (Magicide)*

**The Colon –**

Use a colon before a list.
*Even the names of the effects were magical: Cigarette Through Card, Twisted Sisters, Prayer Vase, The Devil's Bride Illusion. (Magicide)*

Use a colon before a long quotation, especially a formal one.
*Carl Otto showed me where, in the journal he kept for his report to the Governor, he made note of the shorting of several supply lists: "We note that the barrels and chests do not have the weight and size which is assigned to them in the*

*lists that accompanied them. I had four chests opened, which were well nailed down and dry. Found no more than eight or nine jugs' measure inside, yet the list gives each as containing ten jugs' measure. A keg of Society barley, well-sealed and undamaged, is reported on the list as having in it 48 jugs; contains no more than 43 jugs. A barrel which appeared on the list as containing 50 had no more than 40. A barrel of rum which ought to contain 36 contains no more than 10 little kegs." (Elisabeth Samson, Forbidden Bride)*

Use a colon before part of a sentence that explains what has just been stated.
*She remembered Christian's words: This gold rush sweeping the Amazon shows no sign of abating. (Hard Amazon Rain)*

### Ellipsis...
These are the three little dots you sometimes see in the middle of, or at the end of, a sentence. They indicate an intentional omission of a word or phrase. They can also be used in dialogue or first person narrative to indicate a pause.

*"Well, yes... It's also why you can't spend any time alone with me in my house during the day, either." (Hard Amazon Rain)*

*But I digress... I was saying that Maria's wedding to Frederick Coenraad Bosse most impressed me. (Elisabeth Samson, Forbidden Bride)*

*The smell of burning flesh sharpened again in his nostrils. "It was the water...eight villages..." (Hard Amazon Rain)*

### Quotation marks –
We fiction writers all know that quotation marks are used to indicate dialogue.

*Instead she said, "I know it seems wild but this is important to me."*
Notice that in this example the comma is **after** the word said, with a space before the quotation mark. And the period at the end of the sentence is **inside** the quotation mark.

In the following example notice that the comma at the end of the spoken line and before *he said* is **inside** the quotation mark.
*"It doesn't appear that you'll finish your library soon," he said. (Hard Amazon Rain)*

I believe I have just repeated what I said when I talked about where commas go, but this punctuation use is CRITICAL to printed dialogue. It's the accepted standard in print books and what every reader is accustomed to seeing.

Often, when I read manuscripts, I see these commas and quotation marks misplaced.

In first person narrative you may see quotes to emphasize a short descriptive phrase:
*None of the slaves will talk, and Quackoe is unwilling to flog and thus mar valuable merchandise over what he refers to as "the incident." (Elisabeth Samson, Forbidden Bride)*

Notice that in the following two sentences, where I am emphasizing a descriptive word or phrase, the comma is OUTSIDE the quotation mark. This is because the entire sentence is NOT dialogue.
*He'd followed them from Tozario's because he had a "sight", he said.*

*Bon, the "prettier sister", worked as a cocktail waitress on the graveyard shift at the Sultana Hotel/Casino. (Magicide)*

Remember back in chapter 16 I told you that titles of articles, chapters, TV episodes, blog posts, most poems, and other shorter works are enclosed in quotation marks.

*OUTLANDER*, season 1, episode 6: "The Garrison Commander."

**The Semicolon –**
Use a semicolon between closely related independent clauses.
*She would prove to herself she could overcome her fear; she would show mercy on this spider. (Hard Amazon Rain)*

Just for the record, because I don't recommend you use them, here are other semicolon rules:
 - Use a semicolon between main clauses when the coordinating conjunction has been left out.
 - Use a semicolon to join independent clauses when one or both clauses contain a comma.
 - Use a semicolon between main clauses connected by conjunctive adverbs such as however, nevertheless, moreover, for example, and consequently.

The reason I just said I don't recommend you use semicolons is that in fiction you really don't need them. In general, semicolons just tell the reader you went to college and learned something about grammar and punctuation.

Just use two sentences. It's easier on you and your reader.

Here's how I changed that sentence from *Hard Amazon Rain* to eliminate that silly semicolon:
*She would prove to herself she could overcome her fear. She would show mercy on this spider.*

And guess what I just learned while doing confirming research–confirming that I don't know everything after all—for this book?

The word is *semicolon*, not *semi-colon*. No hyphen!

**The Exclamation Point –**
Only one, please!

Using more than one will immediately mark you as an amateur writer!!!

**Do you know the difference between the hyphen and the dash?**
This is a hyphen:  -

The dash (also sometimes called the *em dash*) is longer:
—

In writing fiction, it's a good idea to use the em dash rather than parentheses. Parentheses around words or phrases slow pacing.

*The body of the world's most famous magician—his father—severed in two places, had exploded in a shower of blood and red spandex and rhinestones. (Magicide)*

*She was working the case of a boy's body that had been found in the desert—every hiker's nightmare. (Magicide)*

## CHAPTER 18 – How to do a line edit

Remember back in CHAPTER 7 I told you what a Copy or Line Editor does? To review, s/he looks at every single line of your manuscript with a microscopic eye towards spelling, punctuation and grammar.

You can—and should—do this yourself. At least once, maybe twice. Three times is even better.

I'm going to digress for a minute here to talk about a common grammar error.

I understand that the English language is constantly evolving, but I admit to a "grammar pet peeve."

Not only do I see this in writing, but I hear evening newscasters—even teachers—speaking this way: "Today, people **that** want to donate...", "Every teacher I know **that**..." "I loved the woman **that** sang..."

The correct usage here is "people **who**, teacher **who**, woman **who**."

The grammatical rule is: "**people** who— **things** that—"

So, "who" should be used with words like anyone, someone, no one, teacher—any noun referring to a person. "That" should only be used with objects.

And while we're at it: is there anyone in the internet universe who doesn't know where SPELL CHECK is on a computer?

I've been a magazine editor and a contest judge and recently I've edited other writers' manuscripts. Spelling errors happen too often, and even if they're just typos, they SHOULD NOT BE THERE.

I'm also amazed at the **HOMONYMS** that frequently pop up.

HOMONYMS are words that are often "misspelled" by using a similar word that has its own meaning. Sometimes they're just typos, but sometimes writers— I'll call them "careless" writers rather than "illiterate" writers—don't seem to get the use differences between "you're" and "your", "it's" and "its."

As dear to my dreams as spell check is, it won't save you in the HOMONYM department.

Here are some of the frequent and embarrassing little HOMONYMS you want to proof carefully for:

four and fore
you're and your
it's and its
on and one
their, there, and they're
the and then
here and her
whose and who's
though, through and thought
to and too

Years ago when I was creative manager for a company producing a catalogue, a six-foot (6') grandfather clock was printed as a 6" grandfather clock. Big difference in clock sizes, wouldn't you agree? Five people—including myself—proofed that catalogue and *none* of us caught that typo.

It's easy to miss these things.

I've read that editing is difficult because we don't "read" the entire word. Your brain "sees" a word as a kind of symbol or picture on the page.

The way the brain works is that as we learn words we train neurons to recognize them as complete, not parts of the words. As long as the number of characters are correct and the first and last letter of the word are correct, we will understand it.

Here's an example from www.livescience.com: "It deson't mttaer in waht oredr the ltteers in a wrod aepapr, the olny iprmoatnt tihng is taht the frist and lsat ltteer are in the rghit pcale. The rset can be a toatl mses and you can sitll raed it wouthit pobelrm."

Hmmmm…

A good way to line-edit your manuscript is to take a blank sheet of white paper and place it over the entire typed page except for the bottom line. Read that last line carefully for punctuation and spelling.

Then raise the blank sheet to reveal the line above that. Edit that line by itself.

Continue to edit line by line, moving the blank paper up the page from the bottom. This way you are not distracted by the meaning of what has been written.

You can focus totally on the spelling and punctuation alone.

A final word on PUNCTUATION:

The reason we have accepted styles of grammar and punctuation is to be able to communicate effectively.

Did I mention you can save yourself money by not having to pay an editor to line-edit?

## CHAPTER 19 – Boo-boos that mark you as an amateur

You definitely want to avoid the following boo-boos that mark you as an amateur writer.

This information is adapted from an excellent writing craft book by James V. Smith, *You Can Write a Novel* (1998).

(You also definitely want this book on your craft bookshelf.)

James V. Smith labeled this section: *You might be an amateur if:*

1) You write endless synonyms for said:
*Breathed, sighed, coughed, smiled, laughed (all of these are not ways that we speak)*

2) You use countless –ly words.
*suddenly, abruptly, happily, softly, loudly, creatively, darkly, lightly*

3) You overuse adjectives.

4) You use weasel words.
*Almost, about, appears, approximately, probably, seems, greenish (all –ish constructions)*

5) You rely on clichés.
(Reread chapter 11)

6) You write heavy dialect.

7) You repeat yourself over and over (echo words, echo story).

8) You use passive voice.
(Reread chapter 14)

9) You use a lot of Point of View shifts.
(Reread chapter 3)

Along with clichés, there are some WORDS that automatically brand you as a novice writer.

Rayne Hall, in *Twitter For Writers*, suggests you create your own writing tip sheet listing these words:

*Look, turn, start, begin, could, smile, feel, slowly, suddenly*

This is not to say that these are BAD WORDS. Just be careful how—and how OFTEN—you use them.

## CHAPTER 20 – Here's the NUMBER ONE SECRET you've been waiting for that can immediately "power up" your writing!

It's called **BACKLOADING**!

BACKLOADING is taking the most important word in your sentence, paragraph, scene or chapter and placing it at the end.

BACKLOADING
— puts the psychological weight at the **end** of the sentence and propels the reader into the next sentence—or paragraph or scene or chapter.

— is the simplest and the most powerful editing technique to learn. Once you begin to apply it, you'll realize what a difference it can make.

— helps increase pacing. Many factors in writing slow pacing. Backloading fixes a lot of that.

This concept of putting the most powerful word at the end of a sentence is what comics do when they write one-liners.

Now I personally know a lot of comics and have never heard any of them say the word "backloading." In comedy-speak, it's the "punchline" or "punch word." And, as you'll see in the following famous one-liners, we're talking about the same thing.

Rodney Dangerfield wrote:
*"I looked up my family tree and found out I was the **sap**."*
He didn't write, *"I was the sap in my family tree."*

Mitch Hedberg, known for surreal humor, wrote:
*"I find a duck's opinion of me is very much influenced by whether or not I have **bread**."* He could have written, *"Whether or not I have bread influences what ducks think about me."*

He also wrote, *"What happened when Jesus wanted to **swim**?"* He could have written, *"When Jesus wanted to swim, what happened?"*

Actor and comedian Zach Galifianakis wrote:
*"I have a lot of growing up to do. I realized that the other day **inside my fort**."* He didn't write, *"The other day inside my fort I realized I have a lot of growing up to do."*

Comedian, actor and writer Steven Wright wrote:
*"I think it's wrong that only one company makes the game **Monopoly**."* He could have written, *"I think it's wrong that the game Monopoly is only made by one company."*

Are you getting the idea?

Here are two examples of back-loaded sentences from *Hard Amazon Rain*:
*Not that she cared—she had her own predicament—but this captain had caught her attention and aroused **her sense of danger**.*

I could have written: *Not that she cared—she had her own predicament—but her sense of danger was aroused by this captain.*

*Amid a thrashing splash the dugout **capsized**.*
I could have written: *The dugout capsized amid a thrashing splash.*

The concept of BACKLOADING works with chapter endings as well. It can act as a teaser to draw your reader immediately into the next chapter, instead of putting the book down at that point.

The following sentence from *Hard Amazon Rain* ended the last paragraph of a chapter:
*But her intuition whispered that she'd not **seen the last of Captain Christian St. Cloud**.*

I could have written:
*She'd not seen the last of Captain Christian St. Cloud, her intuition whispered.*

Here's how I ended the last paragraph of a chapter in *Magicide*:
*"You're the police. You get the DVD from Carter. You'll see you're right about one thing — **Maxwell wasn't alone**."*

Many authors use BACKLOADING to make their sentences more powerful. A QUICK CHECK of how well you've backloaded sentences is to circle the last word in each sentence and read it out loud.

Does this mean we can backload every sentence with a power word?

No. Not every sentence lends itself to backloading. But so many sentences do that you will see a significant change in the power of your writing when you apply this simple secret.

## YOUR HOMEWORK ASSIGNMENT, should you choose to accept it:

1) Select one chapter and read EVERY SENTENCE to determine if you can rearrange the sentence to backload it by putting the most interesting word—the POWER word—at the end.

— Can you substitute words or phrases to backload the sentence?

2) Circle the last words of EVERY PARAGRAPH.

— Are they power words?
— Can you rearrange words or phrases to make them power words?

3) Analyze the LAST PAGE of your chapter.

— Does the chapter end at the most effective point?
— Is there a hook?
— Is there anything you can add, subtract or change to power up the backloaded hook?
— Does the last sentence leave the reader "hanging", like the end of a serial TV show, so that the reader must immediately begin to read the next chapter?

Remember – you won't be able to backload every sentence.

But I bet that using this technique, you'll find you can power up as much as THIRTY PERCENT of the total sentences in your fiction writing.

Margie Lawson says, "The reader won't consciously be aware that you've backloaded, they'll just think your writing is strong."

*YES!*

# BONUS – Seven Secrets For Fiction Writing Success

## 1. FIRST, GET READY!

Before you start to write, do as much RESEARCH as possible. This will help you with the details that make a story come alive and may give you ideas for new conflict or scenes.

I personally love research. Especially if I can find a person to interview, to ask all those questions mother told you were not polite to ask. Nothing like getting first-hand insight from someone who actually makes a living in a trade or profession like what your character does.

Think about where and when you will write.

Do you have a quiet, private space in which to work? Or do you need to go to Starbucks or the library? Stephen King suggests that to write without distractions your desk should face a blank wall.

Are you a morning person? A night owl? You know when your energy is highest. That's when you should be writing. I find that I write best first thing in the morning, still in my jammies, with a cup of coffee. For me, just a couple of hours or two thousand words in the morning makes me feel for the rest of the day like I've accomplished something.

If you feel stuck at some point, take a break for a walk or other activity…something more than just a fresh cup of coffee or a trip to the bathroom.

Let your subconscious mind work overnight on a problem or situation, and when you begin writing again, it will flow.

## 2. OUTLINE YOUR STORY

In a writing workshop once, the instructor asked, "Are you a pantser or are you a plotter?"

She explained that a **pantser** just starts writing and lets the story flow "from the seat of his pants." A **plotter** outlines everything in advance, and knows where his story is going.

Being a pantser might sound a lot more "creative" but I believe you'll accomplish a lot more, faster, if you are a plotter.

A great way to construct your story is to outline each individual scene on individual note cards. This process forces you to think logically and choose a chapter order.

Also on each scene card note *action/reaction* and closing paragraph *hook*.

Number one best-selling author James Patterson outlines in detail—sometimes up to eighty pages for each book—before he begins to actually *write*.

Recently, I discovered **Scrivener**, a software program designed especially for screenwriters and fiction writers. It helps you organize your chapters, characters, locations and research (including photos!) all in one place. Everything is super easy to access while you write.

Lots of best-selling as well as aspiring writers are working fans of Scrivener. As I draft my current novel in the program, I'm rapidly becoming a fan, too.

I think Scrivener was the best under-$50 investment I've made in my writing career!

Here's the site where I purchased Scrivener: www.literatureandlatte.com/scrivener.php

Here I need to tell you that I'm not in any way affiliated with them, and receive no commission if you buy the program. I just want to share with you what works well—and fast—for me.


## 3. SHORTER IS BETTER

Shorter words. Shorter sentences. Shorter paragraphs. Especially in action scenes, "shorter" moves the story forward faster and heightens the drama.

Simple, straightforward, non-technical language keeps the pacing steady and keeps the reader engaged.

James Patterson, certainly the most prolific author of our time, has more than 130 completed works. *Vanity Fair* calls him, "a relentless writing machine."

He is the master of *short*.

"Patterson's formula is brutally simple. His books have lots of periods in the paragraphs, lots of paragraphs per page, and very few pages per chapter, as few as three or four." *Vanity Fair, January 2015.*

So what about the right novel length?

For fiction, especially if you are writing your first novel, an accepted word count is 70,000 to 85,000 words.

This is not to say you can't write something shorter. Stuart Woods, one of my favorite fiction authors, writes snappy, action-oriented stories around 60,000 words.

Best-selling "true detective" pulp fiction writers of the 1940s and '50s, and even into the '60s, wrote as few as 50,000 in a book.

Anything shorter than that and you are in "novella" territory, and you need to label your work with that word so as not to disappoint your reader.

Would it surprise you to know that it's harder to write short, crisp fiction than to ramble on and on?

## 4. VISUALIZE YOUR READER

Having an idea of the person most likely to be interested in your story—your "target audience" as we say in advertising—will help you use the most appropriate method and language.

I know you're immediately thinking, "But everyone would like my book."

An advertising adage says, if you are everything for everybody, then you are nothing for anybody. The only product "everybody" would use is toilet paper.

A writing guru I follow is London-based Joanna Penn, a *New York Times* and *USA Today* bestselling thriller author. She's also a professional speaker on creative entrepreneurship, digital publishing and internet marketing.

At her website, www.thecreativepenn.com, she shares *5 Tips on How to Identify Your Target Audience.*

Among her five tips are:
— Identify other books that are comparable to yours and look at the profiles of those books' main buyers.
— Pinpoint what is special about your book.

Check out Joanna's website for her other tips.

She has a lot of good information for both the fiction and the non-fiction writer.

James Patterson—who coincidentally has a long-time successful advertising background with uber-agency J. Walter Thompson—says, "I know who my readers are and how to engage them."

He suggests you imagine that you are telling your story to a woman sitting across the desk from you. He says, "Woman, because seventy percent of novels are purchased by women."

## 5. WRITE, REWRITE AND READ OUT LOUD

Congratulations! You've finished your first draft. Now the real work begins.

Read what you've written from the beginning. You will rewrite and tweak along the way and this will be your second draft.

Now read your story out loud to yourself—or to a patient friend. This will help you identify long passages that may slow the pacing, or places where clarification is needed.

For instance, if you have to take a breath in the middle of a character's dialogue sentence, that sentence is too long.

I have a writer friend who gets another friend to "play out the scene" with her, like a movie script, so she can feel how it would work if her book were someday made into a movie.

When you read your writing out loud, you will "hear" awkward phrasing and discover any spot where you may have repeated words inappropriately.

## 6. REVIEW SPELLING AND GRAMMAR

With spell check and the line editing system I described in Chapter 18, there's NO EXCUSE for you to have misspelled words and bad grammar in your manuscript.

I know two entertainer friends who have written and published books that, frankly, would embarrass me as a writer. As entertainers these two are successful and have a built-in audience to buy their books. They are great storytellers. But neither of them would invest a few hundred bucks to have their labors professionally edited.

Frankly, I don't get it.

Remember, misspelled words and bad grammar mark your work as amateur. It's kind of like not rehearsing for a really important show!

Now really, do you want to be viewed as amateur or professional?

Misspelled words and bad grammar also interrupt the reader's concentration and make it more difficult for him to focus on the story. These things also increase the chance that the reader will not finish reading the book because all these things are just too distracting.

## 7. LEARN THE PROPER PRINT FORMAT

Make sure your book looks professional before you submit it to an agent or self-publish it.

Your credibility is on the line here. Your book represents *you*. If it is not professionally formatted, it will reflect negatively on you AND your writing, even if the content is good and it is well-written.

Think about how you would dress for an important job interview. Would you wear sloppy old clothes and hope the interviewer can see your true, inner potential?

I'm not going to apologize here for the fact that APPEARANCES ARE EVERYTHING. It's who we are as human beings. We DO "judge a book by its cover!" So it's CRITICAL for you to present your labor of literary love in the proper format.

And the proper, accepted format is a Microsoft WORD document with one-inch MARGINS all the way around, with your text in TIMES ROMAN font, 12 point, however other acceptable fonts for fiction are Palatino and Garamond.

And for fiction, you don't want an extra space between your paragraphs. You want to INDENT each paragraph.

Also, when you are typing, there is only ONE SPACE at the end of each sentence, NOT TWO!

Two spaces is left over from the old typewriter days, when courier was the only font. Professional typesetters—now a dead profession—always set the text with only one space at the end of a sentence. And that is the rule today.

Also, typing two spaces immediately signals to editors and agents that you're old! ☺

If you plan to indie-publish your book, both Amazon and Smashwords have clear, concise and easy-to-understand publications on how to format your manuscript for their publication requirements.

Same for Createspace if you plan to indie-publish a paperback version of your novel.

Everything you need to know about how to properly format a book is out there in cyberspace.

Google it!

**Here's BONUS SECRET #8:**

**READ!**

Do you read other fiction books?

I know this sounds like a dumb question, but I do meet people who want to write a book, but don't read. One guy actually told me, "Reading is boring."

So *what* do you read?

Once I asked a wannabe romance writer who her favorite romance authors were. She said, "Oh, I don't read romance. I read science-fiction."

It should go without saying that you should be reading books in the GENRE in which you want to write.

You want to know what else is out there that might be similar to your story. Later you will want to market to people who bought other books like yours.

You want to know if someone else has already used your title. I recently searched for a one-word book title at Amazon.com and found six (!) books with the same title.

A dated writing adage says, "Write what you know."

I say, "Write what you **like**." You'll be far more interested in reading about your favorite subject or genre and doing research to learn more about it.

In *The Elements of Editing* Arthur Plotnik says you can learn a lot by reading "other writers whose choice of words and word arrangement establishes our standards of literate communication."

## IN CONCLUSION

Successful editing and revision requires you to perform three operations, separately or at the same time.

You *can* multi-task, right?

**1 – Ask yourself,** Is this action important to the development of my story?

**2 – Be sure that each reaction is motivated**—and that each motivating stimulus (action) gets a reaction.

**3 – Check your story line by line for clarity and consistency.** To be clear is to be distinct, plain, easily and correctly understood.

**And a final important piece of POWER EDITING advice:**

> If you need to cut a LITTLE,
> cut out FACTS, NOT emotion.

> If you need to cut a LOT,
> cut out SCENES, NOT emotion.

## AFTERWORD

Dear Fiction Writer,

Thank you so much for purchasing *Power Editing For Fiction Writers* and investing your time to read the entire book.

I hope that from reading this editing guide you have gained a focused direction to confidently edit your manuscript and save yourself *beaucoup* bucks.

If you found useful tips and inspiration here, please let me know by rating *Power Editing For Fiction Writers* at amazon.com and writing a brief review. As an indie author, reviews are important for me in order to help other writers find the information I've shared here with you.

Get more writing tips and inspiration FREE from my newsletter, *Secrets of Fiction Writing Success.* You can sign up at my website, www.carolynvhamilton.com

Check out my blog at carolynvhamilton.wordpress.com

Come on over to my page at Goodreads and join the conversation:
www.goodreads.com/Carolyn_V_Hamilton

If you would like to send me a tweet, my twitter address is @AnAdventuress

Now I'm going to go enjoy a glass of wine to toast to your writing, editing and publishing success!

Carolyn

# LIST OF RECOMMENDED RESOURCES MENTIONED IN THIS BOOK

Hollywood screenwriting expert Hal Croasman: http://screenwritingu.com/

Donald Maass, *Writing the Breakout Novel*

Steve Windsor, *Nine Day Novel Writing*

Robert McKee, *Story*

James V. Smith, Jr., *You Can Write a Novel*

Margie Lawson's website, www.margielawson.com

Theodore Rees Chaney, *GETTING THE WORDS RIGHT: How to Revise, Edit and Rewrite*

Layne Hall, *Twitter For Writers*

Arthur Plotnik, *The Elements of Editing*

Stephen King, *On Writing*

Lynne Truss, *Eats, Shoots & Leaves: The Zero Tolerance Approach to Punctuation*

Joanna Penn, http://www.thecreativepenn.com


Here is another writing book I highly recommend:

Noah Lukeman's How-To-Write book, *The First Five Pages*

And be sure to check out the master class, *James Patterson on Writing*

**Reviews are everything!**

If you enjoyed this book, I would really appreciate it if you would go to Amazon, rate the book and write one or two lines about what you liked about this information.

# Carolyn V. Hamilton

My business card says "author, artist, adventuress."

I have written fiction and memoir, I love to lead writing workshops, and I'm also a free-lance journalist.

Professionally trained as an illustrator and graphic designer, I spent over three decades working as a marketing executive and copywriter in the real world of *Mad Men*. My BA, in Liberal Arts, is from Antioch University Seattle.

In 2009 I founded www.adventuress-travel-magazine.com, the digital magazine "for women over 50

oing fun things", focusing on essay stories from women
bout their personal travel adventures.

Ay other adventures have included two years' service as
 U.S. Peace Corps Volunteer and a stint—in my
younger days"—as a Playboy Bunny.

Vhen I'm not traveling, my home base is Cuenca,
 cuador, up in the Andes in South America.

 o learn more, please visit my website at
 vww.carolynvhamilton.com

 f you have any questions about any part of *POWER
 DITING FOR FICTION WRITERS* you can e-mail me
 ersonally at info@carolynvhamilton.com

## Books by Carolyn V. Hamilton

## FICTION

### *Magicide*
*(a murder mystery)*

Maxwell Beacham-Jones, the world's most famous magician, has reached the zenith of his success. Now he's planned the most daring, outrageous trick of his career.

But when Maxwell dies in a Las Vegas roller coaster escape stunt before a national television audience, it's no accident. He was hated by his contemporaries, and all of the suspects are magicians—with plenty of secret motives for murder.

MAGICIDE introduces Las Vegas Metro Police detective and single mom, Cheri Raymer, and her vegetarian partner, Tony Pizzarelli. Together they follow a trail through the world of magic and show business that leads to intrigue and shocking revelations.

Raymer will face the most devastating personal threat in her career when her teen-aged son, Tom, fascinated by magic, becomes the protégé of a suspected killer.

### *Hard Amazon Rain*
*(An eco-adventure romance)*

Burned-out art therapist Dianti Robertson dreams of building a library for an Amerindian village on the upper Amazon in Peru. She's searching for a feeling of ompletion, and the library is a project completely ifferent from her ongoing work with troubled children 1 America.

:oaming the Amazon River, English eco-activist :hristian St. Cloud sails his trimaran, the *Rio Vida*, vherever he perceives a threat to the Amerindian way of fe, opposing those whose greed would strip the people f all their natural resources. Christian is haunted by aving been unable to save nine indigenous villages :om being destroyed by a dam project in Venezuela.

)ianti and Christian strongly disagree on how best to aid idigenous people. Complicating their outspoken ifferences is the intensity of their unspoken physical ttraction.

)utch soldier-of-fortune Kees Wijntuin and a ruthless old consortium threaten the area where Dianti lives. Vhen two young Amerindians are kidnapped by the )utchman and sold into slavery at the mining camp of anto Ignacio, Dianti and Christian must join forces to escue them.

### :lizabeth Samson, Forbidden Bride
*Historical fiction based on a true story)*

1 the 18th century Dutch plantation colony of Suriname, vhere wealth is measured by the number of slaves one wns, the Free Negress Elisabeth Samson, educated and vealthy owner of several flourishing coffee plantations, vants only to marry her true love, a white man.

ut can she overcome the strict Dutch laws forbidding 1arriage between black and white against the powerful forces of the colonial Governor, the white planters who make up the Court of Justice, and the Society of Suriname, who call her whore, covet her property, and accuse her of treason?

## IMPLOSION
*(Mystery)*

With the pending implosion of the grand old Las Vegas hotel/casino, the Desert Palace, an eleven-year-old mystery of six million dollars stolen from the casino count room remains unsolved.

Everyone who has touched the money has died a horrible death, giving rise to the legend that this money is cursed.

Newspaper reporter Nedra Dean feels the pressure to use every means she can to make this dramatic moment in Las Vegas history her biggest scoop, one she hopes will catapult her to big-time journalism at CNN.

Celebrity maitre d' Eduardo only wants to reconcile his estranged family before his forced retirement.

And somewhere, within the walls and floors of the Desert Palace, the cursed six million dollars waits, which owner "Crazy" Foxy Craig is desperate to find before the walls come tumbling down.

# MEMOIR

**Coming To Las Vegas, A True Tale Of Sex, Drugs & Sin City In The '70s**

In 1973 Carolyn Hamilton arrives in Las Vegas with boyfriend Del to join the business side of the newly-formed Las Vegas International Circus. When they run out of money Carolyn gets a job as a cocktail waitress in the soon-to-open MGM Grand Hotel/Casino. Through nefarious means, Del gets the position as bailiff for District Court Judge Paul Goldman. Carolyn and Del marry, but Del's ex-wife surfaces, and he is revealed as a bigamist.

Working cocktails at the MGM turns out to be more involved than a nice Lutheran girl from Seattle would think: rumors, parties, stealing, sex, drinking and drugs are the main entertainment for a bored crew of cocktail waitresses, bartenders, dealers and floormen. Some waitresses date culinary union bosses, who have their own high drama of payoffs, fights for control, fire bombings and an 18-day culinary union strike.

After a *ménage a quatre* with two other waitresses and a casino floorman, Carolyn decides this is not the kind of life she wants for herself. After three years she leaves the MGM to rediscover her personal values and commitment to her marriage.

Each story told in this memoir—of the Martin Scorsese *Casino* era of Las Vegas—is true, and many of them are humorous as well as outrageous.

### *My Mind Is An Open Mouth, A Life Behind the Mic*

With his outlandish, machine-gun rapid-fire humor, comedian Cork Proctor has been knockin' 'em dead for sixty years ... literally. From his first attempt at stand-up comedy as a gravedigger entertaining his co-worker to lounges and showrooms around the world — on land and sea — this left-handed, dyslexic, two-time high school dropout has not only seen it all, he tells it all.


## NON-FICTION

### *Art Improv 101: How to Create a Personal Art Journal*

Art Improv 101: How to Create a Personal Art Journal focuses on creative play. This method is to art what improv is to comedy; You will make it up as you go along.

Based on 30 years in the graphic arts, artist and writer Carolyn V. Hamilton will share with you ways to play with watercolor techniques, shading with pencils, using decorative borders, and tips for drawing faces, trees, and other objects.

Her goal is to inspire you to create your own personal art journal where you can note thoughts, look inward, officially doodle, observe your life, and maybe even realize miracles.

This book contains dozens of technique illustrations. No experience required!